Learning to Learn —
The Fourth Generation

Making Sense of Personalised Learning

Guy Claxton

TLO

An earlier version of this text was published in 2004 as
Teaching Children to Learn by the National Primary Trust.

Published in 2006 by TLO Limited
Henleaze House, Harbury Road, Bristol BS9 4PN

The right of Guy Claxton to be identified as the author
of this work has been asserted by him in accordance with
the Copyright, Designs and Patents Act 1988.

Cover image © Christophe Alary

ISBN   1 901219 52 6

ISBN-13 781 901219 52 4

Contents

1   Introduction 1

2   The First Two Generations 2

3   The Third Generation 3

     G3 approaches to learning to learn 3
         Emotional factors 3
         Learning styles 3
         The 'science' of G3 3
         Beyond G3? 4

     The whole elephant 5

     Learning styles? Old hat 6

     The business of learning-to-learn 7

4   The Fourth Generation 8

     Going transparent 8
         The power of STUCK 8
         Making it their own 10

     The mental gymnasium 10

     'Personalised learning' 11

     Where did the content go? 12
         Skills out of context 14
         Encouraging transfer 14

     A developmental approach to L2L 15

     The L2L curriculum 15

     Dispositions: the adverbs of the mind 16

     Talking and modelling 18

     The L2L school as a whole 20

5   Knitting the Strands of the Fourth Generation Together 21

6   Learning to Learn for Life: the Emerging New Vision for Schools . . 23

References and notes 24

About the Author

Guy Claxton is Professor of the Learning Sciences at the University of Bristol's Graduate School of Education. He is the author and editor of more than twenty books, including the best-selling *Hare Brain, Tortoise Mind*, *The Wayward Mind* and *Building Learning Power*. His practical ideas about how to expand young people's appetite and capacity for learning have influenced educational theory and practice in many countries, including New Zealand, Australia and Brazil, as well as in the UK. He holds degrees from Cambridge and Oxford, and is a Fellow of the British Psychological Society.

Learning to Learn — The Fourth Generation

Making Sense of Personalised Learning

Guy Claxton

1   Introduction

'Learning' seems to be very popular at the moment. Everywhere you go, people are talking about 'personalising learning', 'improving learning', 'lifelong learning', the 'learning society', 'learning to learn' and so on. In 2003, the then Schools Minister, David Miliband, declared that 'learning how to learn in preparation for a lifetime of change' was one of the three core functions of teaching in the twenty-first century.[1] Estyn, the Welsh Schools Inspectorate, has recently insisted that 'schools will need to devote attention to developing ... the dispositions of learners, and their learning skills, as well as to developing formal instruction.'[2] Almost every school prospectus starts with some fine words about 'preparing our young people for a lifetime of learning'. Teachers flock to courses on 'accelerated learning', 'brain-based learning', 'building learning power', 'teaching critical thinking', and the like. There is no doubting the widespread enthusiasm for the idea of 'improving students' learning' throughout the UK — indeed, around the world.

But what exactly is it that everyone is so enthusiastic about? What, in practice, do people mean when they use these fine phrases? And how has teachers' hunger for ideas and information about 'teaching' and 'personalising' learning been met? It is time to take stock of 'learning to learn', and see how the idea has developed, what shortcomings have been rectified, and what remain, and how the idea might be improved still further.

> *... education might be able to deliver more effectively what young people say they want: greater confidence and capability in the face of real-world uncertainty.*

I shall argue that there have, over the last twenty years or so, been three generations of response, each more powerful than the last; and that we are now ready to make a step change into a Fourth Generation approach to helping young people become better learners. Each of these generations is still with us: they overlap and linger, rather than replacing each other in a series of neat revolutions. But there are strong signs that the Third Generation is rapidly metamorphosing into the Fourth; and that, while a good deal of practical wisdom has already accrued, the latest perspectives are opening up a panorama of new possibilities — and new questions. The Fourth Generation is just beginning; but it seems to hold out an important promise: that education might be able to deliver more effectively what young people say they want: greater confidence and capability in the face of real-world uncertainty.[3] I shall pass quickly over what I am calling Generations One and Two, and will focus on the Third Generation, and the ways in which it too is being rapidly superseded.

2   The First Two Generations

The first generation was a recognition of 'learning' in name only. When people said they were interesting in 'improving the quality of students' learning', it rapidly turned out – by page 3 of the prospectus, say – that all they meant was 'raising attainment'. 'Learning' was used solely to refer to the *outcome* of schooling: the Key Stage 2 SATs results, or the A*–C's at GCSE, for example. There was no recognition of 'learning' as an interesting and complicated *process* going on in children's conversations and between their ears. In the first generation, the idea of 'good teaching', therefore, did not need to alter. Good teaching was clear, well-paced, interesting, systematic. It remained defined in terms of the teacher's ability to put across information, and develop the skills of literacy, numeracy and so on, in a pleasant and effective manner.

The second generation of approaches to 'learning to learn' aimed to develop 'study skills'. It was based on a dawning recognition that there were practical things that students could do to improve the organisation of their knowledge, the reliability of their memories, or the effectiveness of their revision. The concern with 'improving learning' usually surfaced before exams, and manifested itself as hints and tips on how best to retain and recall what had been learned. Students were given ideas about how to plan their revision schedule; how to use mnemonics to remember their French irregular verbs or the colours of the rainbow; how to represent the structural relationship of key points using 'spider diagrams', or what came to be branded and commercialised as 'mind maps'. Learning to learn involved practising a few simple techniques that would enhance comprehension, organisation and retention, and thus improve performance in traditional examinations. 'Good teaching' was much as before, but supplemented by the one-off transmission of a few such techniques.

Learning to learn — the four generations

First Generation	Raising attainment Outcome of schooling (e.g. KS2 SATs results) 'Good teaching' was about content and acquisition 'Good teachers' could put across information, develop literacy and numeracy, etc.
Second Generation	Develop study skills Hints and tips on retaining and recalling for tests Practising techniques 'Good teaching' as before, plus delivering these techniques
Third Generation	Expanded to include emotional factors (e.g. self-esteem) Characteristic ways of learning (e.g. multiple intelligences) 'Good teaching' included reducing stress levels and helping students raise their attainment levels Concerned with the 'how' of teaching
Fourth Generation	Involvement of students in the processes Concerned with how students can be helped to help themselves (e.g. think creatively) Teachers themselves involved in becoming better learners Developmental and cumulative – encouraging the 'ready and willing', not just the 'able'

3   The Third Generation

G3 approaches to learning to learn

Emotional factors

The third generation approaches to learning questioned two main aspects of the second: its overwhelmingly cognitive focus (largely on memory); and the reduction of learning-to-learn — L2L hereafter — to simple 'hints and tips' that could be 'bolted on' to classroom practice without changing the teachers' normal *modus operandi*. In the third generation ('G3') approaches, the

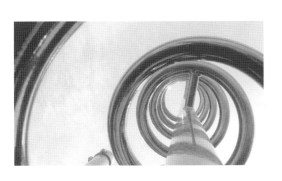

understanding of learning was expanded to include emotional factors such as 'self-esteem'. It became widely believed that children couldn't learn (as well, or at all) if they were stressed, and so 'good teaching' came to include the modulation of the emotional climate in the classroom. Self-esteem, it was thought, could be undermined by the experience of failure, so a 'good' teacher might try to do her best to protect her students from this distress by concealing her (inevitable) judgements of (relative or absolute) failure as much as possible, and by creating gentle gradients of difficulty in the tasks she set, so that children could proceed smoothly upwards without ever getting frustrated or confused — and therefore upset. Various ways of reducing stress levels included playing background music of approved kinds. Mozart would generally be held to be preferable to Gnarls Barkley, for example.

Learning styles

It was also a core article of faith, in G3 approaches, that students possessed enduring 'learning styles' — characteristic ways in which they approached learning as a whole — which were few in number (three, say, or sometimes as many as eight), and relatively easy to diagnose. A popular version of this was the 'VAK' model, according to which all youngsters could be characterised as predominantly Visual, Auditory or Kinaesthetic learners. One local authority booklet on learning to learn for its teachers authoritatively told them that '29% of us prefer to learn by storing [visual] images in our brains', while '34% of us prefer to learn by storing sounds in our brains', and '37% of us prefer to learn by movement or touch'.[4]

A second, rather more sophisticated version of learning styles was based on Professor Howard Gardner's notion of 'multiple intelligences', first published in 1983.[5] Put simply, people possessed not just one fixed, general-purpose pot of 'ability', but eight different ones dedicated to such areas of activity as language, mathematics, music, spatial awareness, physical skill and grace, social relationships, self-awareness, and interaction with the natural world. 'Each of us has all of them,' said Gardner, 'but in different measure and combined in different ways.'[6] The inference that teachers frequently drew was that they should become more aware of the differing profiles of styles and abilities with which they were confronted (by administering approved questionnaires), and expand and diversify their repertoire of teaching methods accordingly. They should remember, for example, to enfranchise the 'kinaesthetic learners', or those richly endowed with 'bodily-kinaesthetic intelligence', by regularly having students move about and touch things. 'Good teaching' expanded again to include ways of engaging these different learning modes and intelligences.

The 'science' of G3

G3 approaches were generally keen to establish their scientific credentials. Teachers were continually provided with seemingly incontestable facts to support the advice they were being given through publications, consultancy and training. '37% of us prefer to learn by movement and touch' sounds pretty confident. 'Research shows that pupils with high self esteem are more successful learners', says the same booklet. Most persuasive of all was the repeated claim that these G3 approaches were underpinned by the latest, cutting-edge research on the brain itself. The booklet from which I have been quoting is subtitled *Get to Know Your Brain and How to Learn*. In the Foreword, the Chief Executive of the LEA tells us that: 'with the advent of highly sophisticated neurological techniques a vast amount of evidence now exists which assists our understanding of how the brain works and how learning really takes place.'

For example, G3 advocates would confidently explain the adverse effect of stress on learning in terms of the workings of the 'reptilian brain', which, under stress, 'blocks the Neo-Cortex and the Limbic System from thinking and remembering, so that learning is slowed down or prevented.' Sipping water while you are studying is justified not solely on the sensible grounds that being thirsty is a distraction, and that being allowed to take a drink when you want to is being treated in a small way like a grown-up, which most children appreciate. No, it is because 'our brains, like the rest of our bodies, become dehydrated if we do not drink enough water. Dehydrated brains cannot learn!' Listening to soothing music, too, has a neuroscientific justification. 'Relaxed brains learn more effectively'. 'Music can help your brain prepare for learning.' And: 'Research shows that playing music by Mozart stimulates the brain.'

There was almost a feeling, in the G3 approaches, that water bottles and background music were so radical, contentious even, that they needed all the support they could get from high-status science — *real* science, not just psychology — to convince teachers and their (assumed-to-be hard-nosed) managers that they were sensible and valid things to do. Many of these G3 approaches were, as I say, greeted with a good deal of enthusiasm. And they did indeed redirect teachers' attention from the traditional preoccupation with content and acquisition — from the 'What?' and 'How much?' of the curriculum — to a genuine interest in the 'How?', and how to support the 'How'.

Beyond G3?

Despite a wealth of enthusiastic anecdotes and endorsements, however, there were few attempts to evaluate the effectiveness of these interventions in any systematic way. But they did begin to get many teachers — and in some cases their students, too — interested in what learning minds were, and how they worked. 'Good teaching' moved beyond the traditional concern with Control and Transmission — with optimising what was going on at the teacher's end of the process — to a recognition that you could not really do that successfully without also thinking about what was going on at the other end, in the hearts and minds of the students. And this required thinking of students not just in terms of the traditional coarse concepts of 'ability' and 'effort' (moderated, in some cases, by 'home background' and/or 'learning difficulties'), but in terms that did greater justice to the real intricacies of learning and thinking. The G3 approaches had their flaws, but they were very effective in preparing the ground for a new wave of approaches, now emerging, that are making yet another step change in our understanding of L2L.

> " *The G3 approaches had their flaws, but they were very effective in preparing the ground for a new wave of approaches, now emerging* "

Over the last few years, it has become apparent that this further development is both necessary, and possible. It is necessary because some cracks have begun to appear in the shiny rhetoric of the G3 approaches. And it has become possible to move on because a deeper and more robust understanding of L2L has been generated by those who had a better grasp of what was actually going on in neuroscience, cognitive science, and other disciplines such as cultural psychology that were contributing fresh ideas to educators about the nature of learning. Perhaps I can summarise these trends by exploring a few ways in which we might judge L2L approaches, and in the light of which we can see the progress that G3 approaches have made over the earlier ones, and also discern where they, in their turn, can be improved upon.

The whole elephant

G3 approaches to L2L tended to be rather bitty. There were plenty of practical ideas around, but they lacked a framework that would make those ideas add up to more than the sum of their parts. Mind maps were supposed to help you organise and retrieve your knowledge; your bottle of water lubricated your brain cells; your learning style told you what your overall learning strengths were, and encouraged you to play to them ... but where was the Big Picture?

If you go down to the local gym, your fitness instructor will have a useful 'map' in her head of what the different elements of 'fitness' are, and how they fit together. The flexibility of your joints, the strength of your limbs, your speed and stamina, the speed of recovery of your respiratory and cardiovascular systems, and your body-mass index: all contribute to fitness. Different exercises, and different bits of kit, help you work on the different elements; and you have an idea of how the stretches and the weights and the running all fit together. Because she has an overview of 'fitness', she can design a balanced and coherent programme for you. But the G3 approaches to L2L were not at that stage. They laid the ground, but they did not have a Big Picture of what the all-round effective learner looked like. So one clear goal for the Fourth Generation approaches is to develop at least a sketch of what overall 'learning fitness' comprises.

Without that overview, some G3 enthusiasts were inclined to mistake the part for the whole — as in the old story of the group of blind people encountering an elephant for the first time. One happened to get hold of the trunk, and declared that elephants were like pythons. Another felt an ear, and claimed that they were not like snakes at all, but like palm leaves. A third grabbed a leg, and asserted that both her colleagues were mistaken: elephants were much more like tree trunks. And so on. (There is a nice version of this story in which a teacher described the situation without telling the children that the people were blind, and asked them at the end what kind of people they thought they were. One child ventured: 'Please, Miss ... experts?') So some teachers and pundits discovered mind maps, and tried to make them the be-all and end-all of L2L. Others got hold of 'self-esteem', or 'learning styles', or 'critical thinking', or 'metacognition', and encouraged their students to develop a lop-sided view of themselves as learners. Fourth Generation approaches would need to make sure that they really were developing 'The Compleat Learner', and not leaving their students with the mental equivalent of over-developed biceps but no stamina.

It is becoming apparent that some of the proponents of G3 learning-to-learn were rather credulous when it came to the scientific underpinnings of their advice. It simply isn't true that the brain can be cloven horizontally into three layers, the lowest of which has the mind and the morals of a snake; nor vertically into two halves, the hemispheres, that do different but complementary mental jobs. Ask someone to read a sentence, or do a simple sum, and within a hundredth of a second both sides of their brain are lighting up all over the place. If they have to say True or False to '2 + 2 = 5' different bits of both right and left hemispheres light up than if you give them 'Two plus two equals five'. Howard Gardner, much respected and much quoted by G3 enthusiasts, has written:

> I do not impugn their motives — though I do question the judgment of the brain's great dichotomisers. Many, for example, sincerely detect faults in our society, especially in its educational system, and are eager to use any method at their disposal to bring about desired changes. But the scientific enterprise is too precious to be sacrificed to any cause, however worthy it may appear. It is time for investigators conversant with brain lateralization to announce that the unknowns in the field dwarf the little that is known, and the little more that is suspected.[7]

Amen to that.

Learning styles? Old hat

Gardner is also in despair about the way his own work on 'multiple intelligences' has sometimes been trivialised or misrepresented by enthusiastic G3 practitioners. In 1999 he published a whole book dedicated to correcting these misunderstandings, in which he comments: 'I once watched a series of videos in [which] I saw youngsters crawling across the floor, with the superimposed legend "Bodily-Kinesthetic Intelligence." I said, "That is not bodily-kinesthetic intelligence; that is kids crawling across the floor. And I feel like crawling up the wall!"' He quotes approvingly an equally exasperated colleague who once quipped: 'Multiple intelligence is a way of saying that you are doing something new, so that you don't *really* have to do anything new.'[8]

A 1997 article by Professor Robert Sternberg, another eminent American researcher, noted that: 'People are probably not "types" ... but rather vary continuously and somewhat differently as a function of diverse person-situation interactions.'[9] In other words, we are all much more variable than the dumbed-down notion of 'learning styles' would have us believe. And what is more, Sternberg concludes: 'Styles, like abilities, are not etched in stone at birth. They appear to be largely a function of a person's interactions with the environment, and they can be developed and socialized.'[10] So the idea that we can find out someone's general-purpose 'learning style' is debunked; and the idea that having done so, we then have to treat it as immutable, and teach them as if they were always and everywhere a 'visual learner', or had 'a high level of logical-mathematical intelligence' is not only false but pernicious. It locks students in to a limited view of themselves, rather than encouraging them to grow.

And indeed students themselves know how contentious the idea of fixed learning styles is. Caroline Lodge at the London Institute of Education has recorded one group of students reflecting on their own teachers' rather naïve notion of learning styles.[11]

Linda: *When they ask you about what style of learning do you prefer – do you like to listen better or do you learn visually – and you don't think about that every day. You don't think when you are in an English lesson, 'Oh I'm listening – "auditory".*

John: *... that's how I learn ...*

Linda: *... and then you are expected to just tell the teacher 'Oh, I learn by listening', and you don't know, you don't think about it.*

Jamie: *You use all of them. It depends on the lesson. It's like a music lesson, you're going to listen aren't you?*

Linda: *Art lesson, you're going to look.*

Jane: *Or if you're given a film to watch in English, you're going to watch it aren't you?*

Jamie: *You're not going to listen to the numbers in the maths lesson!*

[laughter]

A 2004 detailed research review funded by the Learning and Skills Research Centre has concluded that: 'the idea of a learning cycle, the consistency of visual, auditory and kinaesthetic preferences, and the value of matching teaching and learning styles, are all highly questionable.' Indeed, 'some of the best known and [most] commercially successful instruments have such low reliability, poor validity and negligible impact on pedagogy that we recommend that their use in ... practice should be discontinued.'[12]

The business of learning-to-learn

The fact that G3 approaches to learning to learn have sometimes been guilty of exaggeration or naïvety does not mean that the whole project of trying to help young people become better learners is doomed: far from it. Such lapses and excesses are part of the growing pains — the adolescence, if you like — of any worthwhile educational innovation. But it does mean that Fourth Generation practitioners need to be more circumspect, and more critical, about some of the pseudo-scientific claims that are bandied about by the persuasive (and increasingly pervasive) L2L salesmen and women who come knocking on their school's front door.

They must trust their common sense more, and their need for the thin coat of glossy 'brain-based' rationale less. It does not take a PhD in biology, for example, to realise that the human brain, like that of most other creatures, has probably figured out, after thousands of generations of evolution, how to keep itself moist for an hour. And a healthy scepticism about the claims of a CD of classical music called *Baroque-A-Bye-Baby (Sleeptime music for building baby's brain)* is amply justified by the findings of independent research.[13] One of the problems with the G3 approaches was how fast they became appropriated by an army of trainers, entrepreneurs and consultants, with their inevitable branding, sloganeering and over-simplification. Facile little phrases and formulae — 'brain-based learning', 'feel good, learn good' — were thrown around with an air of total profundity and certainty.

Along with these sporadic lapses of critical common sense, G3 practitioners sometimes colluded with the commercialised providers in demanding 'convenience food', or 'flat-pack' versions of L2L: materials that they could simply photocopy and roll out in the classroom without involving either themselves or their students in *thinking* about the issues involved. Perhaps through a lack of confidence, or maybe just a lack of time, teachers provided a ready market for the scores of instant, over-confident, 'How To' manuals that poured off the presses; and for the Quick-Fix courses and seminars that skated in a rapid and often highly entertaining manner over the surface of learning — the charismatic presenter long gone before any doubts or deeper questions had time to bubble to the surface.

There was always something slightly ironic, in some of the G3 approaches, in seeing teachers enthusiastically talking the language of learning, while presenting the ideas they had picked up in a highly rigid and formulaic fashion, as if they were the last word. (Every so often, after a talk, I am still bearded by an agitated, even angry, teacher who cannot understand why I should have been so perverse as to raise doubts about her favourite technique.)

As the ideas of L2L become more familiar, and practitioners gain in confidence and experience, so the Fourth Generation approaches will naturally become less deferential, less 'by-the-book', and more creative, with teachers taking the ideas and principles and making them their own, customising and embellishing techniques to suit the unique conditions of their own classrooms.

4   The Fourth Generation

Going transparent

As teachers develop greater confidence to approach L2L in a critical and creative spirit, so, too, they are coming to involve their students in these processes of appraisal and adaptation. In general, G3 approaches still tended to focus on how the teacher could 'teach' better, rather than on how students could be helped to become better learners. In many of the G3 approaches, ideas and methods for L2L were delivered to the students ready-made. They were presented — like much else in the curriculum — as unequivocally valid and useful, requiring learners only to put them into practice. Students were more likely to be shown a few 'here's one I prepared earlier' mind maps and told what a good idea they were, than to be engaged in a vigorous debate about how best to represent knowledge for various purposes, and how much individual habits and preferences should be allowed to over-ride such generalised advice.

In Fourth Generation approaches, such transparency and student participation are becoming more common. Instead of simply dishing out more good advice to students-as-consumers, classrooms are becoming places of day-by-day *knowledge-generation* about learning, with students being involved, in all kinds of ways, in discovering for themselves, both individually and collectively, what the ingredients of 'good learning' are, and how best they can help themselves to develop. Let me give two examples — displayed in the panels opposite — of how Fourth Generation and G3 approaches to the same resource might differ.

> " *Instead of simply dishing out more good advice to students-as-consumers, classrooms are becoming places of day-by-day knowledge generation about learning.* "

The power of STUCK

Let me unpack the second example a little more. There are a range of different ways of 'mapping' the different elements of all-round learning fitness, but some of those elements are widely agreed. They include

- *resilience* — the habit of persisting with difficulty;

- *resourcefulness* — the ability to deploy a variety of learning strategies;

- *reflection* — the disposition to think about one's own learning, and about oneself as a developing learner; and

- *reciprocity,* or sociability — the ability to learn well in the company of others.[14]

STUCK posters, simple though they are, if used persistently, have an effect on all these four aspects of 'learning power'. Obviously, explicitly, they increase resourcefulness: students have more ideas at their disposal about things they can try. Reflection is stimulated as students are challenged to think about how they can support their own learning. Reciprocity is developed as the elaboration of the posters is a communal activity, subject to continual debate, and the source, often, of a degree of pride in their own ingenuity.

And, slightly less obviously, resilience is strengthened too. When 'being stuck' becomes something that is routinely acknowledged and talked about, and where it becomes a site of potential interest — where a new aid to independence might reveal itself — stuckness stops being interpreted by students as a sign of inadequacy. In many classrooms, being stuck, or even having to try, is interpreted by students as a reflection of their own relative lack of 'ability'. Many students wrongly believe that 'being bright' means never having to break sweat, and never finding learning hard. 'Only stupid people would have to try (at this).' Where these unspoken assumptions are rampant, students tend to shy away from challenge and select easy tasks (so they will not risk looking stupid), or adopt a range of other face-saving strategies.[15]

Learning style questionnaires

In G3, learning styles questionnaires were frequently taken by the teacher as a prompt to change her own teaching style, and by the students as revealing truths about their own learning nature. The presumed goal was to optimise the fit between teaching and learning styles – to connect the two ends of pipe, as it were – so that information transfer happened as smoothly and reliably as possible. A good deal of the work of change was done privately by the teacher, as she planned her forthcoming lessons and wrote Post-its to herself to remind her to 'connect' with the visual learners or those with high interpersonal intelligence.

In the Fourth Generation approaches, a teacher might well use the same questionnaire as a stimulus, but then involve the students in evaluating the results in terms of their own experience, or in designing a small-scale research project to see whether the taxonomy applied to their family and friends. (As a result of this, poor Howard Gardner is now regularly bombarded with emails from UK primary schools asking his views on a new kind of intelligence that appears to have surfaced in Cardiff or Warrington.) Of course the ideas of seven-year-olds will not be as sophisticated as those of a Harvard professor: that is not the point. The point is the students are learning to observe accurately and think creatively about their own habits and processes of learning – and that, reliably, leads to better results and also, often, to greater confidence and capability in learning of all kinds.[16]

THINGS TO TRY IF YOU GET STUCK:

- Ask a friend
- Read the question again
- Use a number line
- Split the question up
- Ask yourself – What do I know already that could help me?
- Use a reference book
- Use a dictionary
- Check the internet
- Share the problem
- Go for another question and come back to the bit you are stuck on later

The STUCK poster: a multi-purpose L2L tool

The second example is the increasingly widespread use of what have come to be called 'STUCK posters'. They come in various shapes and sizes, but essentially they are simply home-made lists of what students can try when they get stuck with their learning: 'Read the question again', 'Split the question into smaller bits', 'Try sounding the word out letter by letter', 'Ask your neighbour' – that kind of thing. If the teacher were simply to photocopy the list from a L2L manual and stick it on the wall, it would be a G3 move. But in a Fourth Generation classroom, the ideas are generated by the students themselves, and are the subject of continual debate and refinement.

Students are challenged to produce a continual stream of ever more sophisticated ideas about how they can boot-strap their own ability to be independent learners, and these are accumulated and displayed as ever-expanding public records of their achievement. To begin with, the teacher trains the students to make use of this information by greeting every request for prompting with; 'Have you looked at the poster?' After a while, looking at the poster becomes routine, and eventually, when the habit of self-unsticking becomes second nature, even the poster becomes redundant. It does not take long, in such a Fourth Generation L2L classroom, before 'Ask the teacher' becomes a last-ditch strategy, to be engaged only when all else has failed.

By contrast, when effort becomes seen as natural and interesting, the habit of perseverance expands, and a subtle but powerful shift in the classroom atmosphere begins to occur.[17] It is in this kind of way that Fourth Generation L2L moves up a gear, from the technical to the cultural. In a sense the STUCK poster is a stand-alone technique, but it can be much more than that if the teacher wants it to be. It can be used as an effective, low-risk, low-investment lever for creating a shift in students' sense of what is valued, what is normal, and what is the point of their learning — and thus in the quality of their engagement.

> *" ... when effort becomes seen as natural and interesting, the habit of perseverance expands. "*

Making it their own

The way Fourth Generation teachers have adapted devices such as the STUCK posters is also telling. Instead of taking the idea and reproducing it verbatim, all kinds of creative customisation has taken place. Over the last five years, 60–70 Cardiff teachers a year have undertaken a small 'action research' project in their classrooms, exploring one aspect of Fourth Generation L2L. One of those teachers dreamed up an acronym for 'stuck', and told her children that STUCK stood for 'Stop – Think – Use Clues Kids'. Within a fortnight the bush telegraph had seen various versions of this acronym appearing in a dozen schools.

Another member of the Cardiff group (with the help of her children) converted the poster into a display of 'Harry's Helpful Hints', capitalising on the popularity in her class of the Harry Potter stories. A third turned the exploration of 'knowing what to do when you don't know what to do' into a version of *Who Wants To Be A Millionaire*, in which her children thought up an ever more ingenious list of 'lifelines'. 'Phone a friend' became 'Ask your learning buddy'. 'Ask the audience' became 'Let's stop and ask the whole class'. 'Go 50–50' was converted into 'See if you can split the problem into smaller bits'. Such ingenuity seems to be the hallmark of Fourth Generation approaches to L2L.

> *" ... the teachers ... are keen to be learners themselves. "*

It is worth noting another Fourth Generation feature that is at the heart of the 'Cardiff Project'. Not only are the teachers being creative, and involving their students in the creative process; they are also being methodical about checking 'what works'. No longer bamboozled by the hype of G3, they are keen to be learners themselves. They don't take the ideas on trust; they design small interventions and take before and after measures in order to see clearly what is really happening. And more power to the LEA for supporting their commitment, both financially and with some expert help in how to carry out such small-scale research projects.[18]

The mental gymnasium

Maybe it will help to make clear what the essence of this climate change is if I develop the 'fitness' analogy that I used earlier in a little more detail. Suppose that students thought of their classroom not simply as a place where they absorbed 'knowledge, skill and understanding', but as a kind of 'mental fitness centre' where they went to spend time with a 'learning-power coach' who would help their minds become stronger and more supple (just as they would go to the gym to be given things to do that would help their bodies get stronger and fitter).

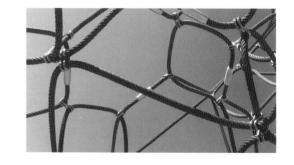

In the physical realm, it is obvious that (a) to make use of the gym, you first have to believe that it is *possible* to get fitter; and (b) you have to realise that getting fitter entails getting hot and sweaty and tired. If you believed that your current level of fitness was essentially fixed — preordained by your genes — then going to the gym would appear to you to be completely pointless. Worse than that, every time you found yourself getting pink in the face and out of breath, you could not but experience this as an unwelcome reminder of how (relatively) unfit you are (and are destined to remain). Happily, most of us hold the contrary belief. Even though I am never going to achieve the strength of a Steve Redgrave or the speed of

a Kelly Holmes, that doesn't mean it is a waste of time my doing a few sit-ups and 15 minutes on the treadmill. And when I do do these exercises, I understand that the whole point is to stretch my system — because that is how I get fitter — and that I know when I am pushing myself precisely because I am finding it hard.

Likewise in school. We know now that 'learning is learnable' to a much greater extent than we had previously thought; and that this expandability of young people's minds is a much more salient and interesting feature than any hypothetical upper limit of 'ability' they might possess. The teacher as learning-power coach tries to get all her students to understand that operating at the current limit of their 'learning power' is exactly where they ought to be, not because this will reveal something eternal about how big their mental capacity ('intelligence') is, but because that is where they will be stretching their minds — and that is where they will be getting 'value for money' out of their education 'membership'.

The analogy of 'school as a learning gym' represents a profound shift in the attitude of schools to their clients. Some children come to school having already spent time in the 'mental gymnasium' at home. They will have been stretched — and more than that, they will have got used to being stretched, and to appreciating and enjoying the process (not all the time, of course — we all need to rest — but regularly). Others, less fortunate, will not have developed their mental stamina and their mental muscles so well, and their tolerance for challenge will be less. But just as we all inhabit some temporary point in the multi-dimensional space of 'physical fitness', so all students are at some point on a developmental trajectory in terms of their mental fitness, their 'learning power'. We all have 'learning difficulties' — the headteacher and the Secretary of State for Education included — and we can all think of ourselves as improving learners, if we want. We can all learn to reframe the symptoms of operating at the outer edge of our current level of fitness — confusion, frustration, stuckness — as signs that we are 'in the zone' where our learning can get better.

'Personalised learning'

This attitude gives some much-needed substance to the current interest in 'personalised learning'. As I say, we all inhabit a temporary point in 'fitness space', where we are comfortably competent; and around that point is our unique, individual 'exercise zone', where we feel stretched and unsure of our ability to cope smoothly and successfully with the challenge in hand. Only I can know where my exercise zone is; and I only know where it is by trying things out, and seeing which of them produce the mental and emotional equivalents of getting hot and sweaty.

❝ The trouble is, sir, the rest of it is all watered-down stuff. ❞

The sports coach sets her trainees tasks that are at the leading edge of their current capacity, and she can only know where that is in collaboration with the trainees themselves. Likewise, the learning-power coach has to watch and listen to her students, and help them — when they are not able to do it for themselves — to select and construct challenges that will give them a satisfying kind of stretch.

> *A group of very average 14-year-old boys in Hamilton, New Zealand, suddenly had the opportunity to work for three whole days on a self-selected science challenge. The energy and ingenuity they showed their teacher was extraordinary. At the end of it, one of the boys, tired but delighted, said rather ruefully, of his normal school experience: 'The trouble is, sir, the rest of it is all watered-down stuff.'[19]*

If 'personalised learning' is to mean anything, it surely must refer, not to a hand-picked diet of topics, let alone a computer-picked programme of tests and tasks, but to this kind of individually tailored exercise regime.

The mental fitness analogy reminds us that not all activity is exercise; not all learning, even when engaged in enthusiastically and productively, is mind-stretching. The fact that students are interested and on task is not enough. They may be learning lots of things, but that does not mean they are learning how to be better learners. G3 teachers' approaches to L2L tended to focus on the question

*How can I help students **learn better?***

rather than, as Fourth Generation teachers' approaches seek to, on

*How can I help them become **better learners?***

Let me ask you to take a moment to sense the gulf between these two questions. It is critical to the distinction between G3 and the Fourth Generation. If my goal is the former, I'm looking for ways in which I can help students master the content more easily and reliably. And that may send me looking for ways in which I can structure the material better, make it more interesting, give clearer and more detailed feedback, and so on. But none of that need leave my students with a heightened sense of their own capability as learners. On the contrary, they might come to rely on my 'good teaching' so much that they are lost when they move on. I might, for instance, make my classroom so cosy and safe that, though my KS2 SATs results are brilliant, I have achieved them at the cost of creating students who are all the more vulnerable when the context is less congenial. I can get my tomato plants to produce a better crop if I put them in the greenhouse, but if I want hardier tomato plants — ones that will thrive when they are planted out — too much cossetting is exactly the *wrong* thing to do.

That, incidentally, is why I insist on referring to the teacher, clumsily, as a 'learning-power coach' — because calling her just a 'learning coach' does not distinguish between these two perspectives. If you just think of yourself as a learning coach, you can be satisfied with the G3 goal of helping students raise their attainment on the conventional indicators. But if you really want to help them become better learners — more resilient, resourceful, reflective and reciprocal, in school *and out* — then I think you have to use the more cumbersome term.

Where did the content go?

This might be the point to scotch two persistent misunderstandings about L2L, at least in its more mature manifestations. The first is that it is a thinly disguised attempt to revert to the bad, muddle-headed, romantic old days of 'child centred' and *'laissez-faire'* approaches to education. Such approaches were said, with a degree of truth, to be driven by a naïve Rousseauesque ideology of childhood, in which all discipline was an insult to the child's spirit, and freedom was a sufficient condition for successful development.

This is, of course, a ridiculous idea, and one with which Fourth Generation learning-to-learn has no truck. Helping young people become better learners inevitably involves giving them increasing amounts of involvement in planning and evaluating their own learning — you'll obviously never learn to think for yourself if someone else is always thinking for you. But you have to be very dim-witted indeed not to see the difference between this gradual, judicious, well-supervised and well-motivated process, and the total abrogation of adult responsibility of which right-wing hysterics like to accuse anyone who dares to innovate.

" ... content and process are not opposed; they are woven together like the warp and weft of cloth on a loom."

The other misconception — again, to be fair, invited by some of the more extreme advocates of earlier generations of L2L — is that paying explicit attention to the process of learning must necessarily mean, at the least, a neglect of content, and at the worst, a rampant anti-intellectualism which would cheerfully ditch Shakespeare and Newton for an unremitting diet of apparently contentless, free-floating 'learning skills'. At one level this is, as I say, a fairly straightforward misconception, for it supposes that content and process must necessarily vie for attention, and that giving more emphasis to one means that the other will inevitably suffer.

But content and process are not opposed, like the two scale-pans on a balance; they are woven together like the warp and weft of cloth on a loom. You cannot teach any topic without presenting it in a way that invites some kinds of learning and not others, and thus exercises and strengthens one set of learning muscles rather than another. For example:

- Traditional chalk-and-talk invites accurate transcription and strengthens the muscles of verbatim retention.

- A seminar discussion recruits and stretches the muscles of real-time argument and interpersonal debate.

- Essay-writing develops the ability to structure an argument at leisure, and to reflect on and revise drafts.

- Factual multiple-choice tests exercise the skill of spotting and rejecting implausible alternatives — as one frequently witnesses in the think-aloud agonising of contestants on *Who Wants to Be a Millionaire.*

And so on. Fourth Generation L2L simply tries to be explicit about the learning-muscle groups that are being targeted, and to take a wider view than traditionalists do of what 'learning fitness' involves.

Actually, even that may not be fair to intelligent traditionalists. In July 2006 actor Stephen Fry gave a much-publicised lecture to launch a campaign for 'good history teaching' called 'History Matters — pass it on'. This was widely seen as a 'back to basics' clarion call, but actually it was nothing of the sort. Towards the end of his speech, Fry said:

> *In the end, I suppose, history is all about imagination rather than facts ... We have to remember what it is like to be a Roman [or] a Jacobite ... If you cannot feel what our ancestors felt ... then all you can do is judge them ... If we dare to presume to damn them with our fleeting ideas of morality, then we risk damnation from our descendants for whatever it is that we are doing that future history will judge as intolerable and wicked: eating meat, driving cars, appearing on TV, visiting zoos, who knows?*[20]

For Fry history matters not because we know of the past, but because it is a prime vehicle for developing powers of imagination and empathy that help people learn from the present and prepare for the future. To be able to put yourself in others' shoes, and to imagine things different from the way they are, opens your mind, and reduces the chance that you will fall into the non-learning pitfalls of dogmatism and righteousness. That is what the Fourth Generation L2L approaches are about. Content is chosen precisely because it is good for exercising valuable learning muscles.

Skills out of context

Where people *have* tried to rip the content and the process of lessons apart, and to teach 'thinking skills', for example, as if they were a topic in their own right, the result has usually been disappointing. The novelty of 'thinking about thinking' usually excites some interest, but anything that has been learned in such lessons mostly fails to re-embed itself back into specific content domains, and simply does not come to mind when it is needed.[21] And indeed, as Chris Woodhead and others have pointed out, there is something rather absurd about abstracting out some desirable-sounding set of psychological 'core competencies' or 'key skills', and imagining that they can simply be trained and reinserted into the mind like a RAM upgrade.

Can we partial out such so-called skills as 'managing personal and emotional relationships', or 'handling information', or 'problem-solving', train them and assess someone's level of attainment? I have some sympathy with Woodhead when he wonders, rhetorically: 'Have I learnt "systematically to think" or "to love learning for its own sake"?', and replies, sensibly: 'No, but I have learnt to think systematically *in some contexts.*[22] Can we assume that the development of a 'disposition to persist in the face of difficulty' in the context of my violin practice will helpfully manifest itself when I am struggling to change a punctured tyre on the hard shoulder of the M4 on a rainy night? No, of course not. And yes, some G3 approaches to learning to learn have grievously underestimated the extent to which mental skills and dispositions tend to stay tied to the contexts in which and the purposes for which they were originally acquired. We develop our abilities to deal with the specific world in which we find ourselves, and do not automatically peel away those details to expose a shiny general-purpose 'skill', ready to be applied whenever it is theoretically relevant.

> *If you want a useful ability or attitude to spread, talk about it.*

Encouraging transfer

However — and here is where the Fourth Generation improves on the Third, and meets the Woodhead criticism — there are ways of teaching that encourage *degrees* of disembedding: not instant and not total, but degrees. And the teaching strategy that is most effective in developing such transferability is explicit articulation and discussion of the skill or disposition in question. If you want a useful ability or attitude to spread, talk about it.[23] So to talk of disembedded L2L qualities such as 'persistence', 'reasoning' or 'seeking connections' is not absurd (a 'mishmash of tautology and gobbledegook', as Woodhead calls it), but neither is it as easy to cultivate them as much of the current rhetoric of generic 'skills' would have us believe.[24]

Again the analogy with physical fitness can help. Any strenuous activity produces change at a number of levels. When you practice your driving on the golf range, you are developing (hopefully) the specific ability to use that particular club. But you are also developing something rather more general called your 'swing'; and something more general still that is to do with the flexibility of your hips and shoulders. At the same time you are 'learning' something quite specific, and also developing elements of your all-round fitness that might indeed have all kinds of unexpected pay-offs, such as an improved ability to twist your head round and look out of the rear window when you are reversing the car.

Remember, however, as I noted above, that not all forms of activity contribute equally, or at all, to the development of overall fitness. In trying to capture a scene in a watercolour I am learning a lot, but the brush-strokes don't make me fitter. Conversely, running on the treadmill works my cardiovascular and respiratory systems very well, but it does not teach me much in the way of useful new specific skill. So it is an open question, at least for the moment, what kinds of classroom activities make the most contribution towards the development of a supple learning mind. Though we don't have all the answers, it is nevertheless the right question to be asking.

A developmental approach to L2L

And that brings us to the next way in which L2L has matured beyond the G3 approaches.

Fourth Generation approaches are explicitly developmental and cumulative.

Only a few years ago, the assumption seemed to be that teachers could acquire most of what they needed to know to 'do L2L' by attending an attractively-presented day workshop (in the company of around 200 other people). You took part in some interesting exercises, bought the manual at the end of the day, and went back to school. They told you the 'five ways to build self-esteem', or the 'best group-work strategies', but what they didn't tell you was how to build L2L week upon week, term upon term, year upon year, so that it stayed fresh, grew ever richer and more sophisticated, and cumulatively, systematically transformed students' weaker habits of mind into stronger ones.

This cumulative goal is, as the new grammar would have us say, a big ask. It demands nothing less than a new approach to development, one that places children's development *as learners* at the centre of our understanding of what growing up is all about. While the old 'intelligence' framework was firmly in place, such a view of childhood was effectively blocked. If most of a child's ability was preordained, there was clearly little point in trying to cultivate it. But now that we know just how learnable learning is — and how dubious the old IQ story is — we are realising that there is a vacancy for this long-term learning-power perspective on development.[25] We know something about children's physical, moral, emotional and intellectual development. We know that some concepts are too hard for small children to grasp. But we don't yet have a good route map of how their learning power grows.

Fourth Generation approaches at least recognise the gap, and many teachers are actively exploring — in collaboration with their students — what the sequences and stages of L2L development might be. They are asking, for example,

- What does resilience mean to a four-year-old, and how can it be appropriately stretched?

- How would the answers to those questions be different if we were talking about 15-year-olds instead?

- Is it possible to get a Year 1 class to reflect on their own learning, and what would that mean to them?

- And if such a process has been started, and carried through, what are those children capable of, as they go up to their secondary schools, that they would not otherwise have been?

As I say, such questions are only just beginning to be addressed. But that beginning makes a big difference. (That's why, in my own attempt to formulate a Fourth Generation approach to L2L, I have laid explicit emphasis on the cumulative process of 'building' learning power.)[26]

The L2L curriculum

> *What special role does each subject, or topic, have to play, when looked on as a specialised piece of equipment or a particular set of exercises in the mental gymnasium?*

Another development in L2L which is similarly just a gleam at the moment is how to link up children's experiences in the 'mental gymnasium' laterally, across different areas of their experience, as well as vertically, over time. And this takes us back to the vexed subject of subjects.

The question that immediately arises is: do different subjects and topics lend themselves to developing different, complementary aspects of mental fitness? Crudely, can we look at physics like we look at the lathe, or, to revert to the earlier metaphor, the cross-trainer in the gym? And at English like the stepper, and maths like the dumb-bells, and art like the stretches and lunges? In other words, how does the curriculum as a whole add up to a comprehensive work-out for the mind? What special role does each subject, or each topic, have to play, when looked on as a specialised piece of equipment, or particular set of exercises, in the mind gym? Stephen Fry argued that history is good for developing imagination and empathy. Can we extend his perspective to the curriculum as a whole?

Seen this way, the 'inherent worthwhileness' of a subject or topic is not a good enough justification for including it in the curriculum. When we ask what special form of mental exercise does this subject demand, some traditional subject-matter might struggle to hold its place. Does adding fractions, an activity that has limited real-world value, nevertheless justify its place in the mathematics syllabus on the grounds that it exercises mental muscles that no other subject does? What kind of stretches are afforded by the study of the Vikings that are not better provided by studying the 1994 holocaust in Rwanda? There is no point in cluttering up the gym with venerable old machines if others will do the job better, or exercise more muscle groups at the same time.

From this functional perspective, some interesting overlaps and alliances between traditionally separate subjects begin to emerge.

- Both scientists and poets need the skill, and the disposition, for meticulous, sometimes very slow and patient, observation. They sometimes need the ability to suspend thinking in the interests of more detailed seeing. So could English and Biology find new ways to join forces?

- Both mathematics and history involve the ability to be inductive: to seek and detect underlying patterns that recur across seemingly disparate episodes and events — could they work together to help young people disembed not just particular patterns, but the very processes and skills of pattern-detection?

At a much more general level,

- What kinds of learning engagement are afforded by any topic at all?

Harvard's Professor David Perkins has recently contrasted what he calls 'wild' and 'tame' topics. Wild ones are full of interesting unexplored possibilities — they stimulate many questions and explorations, and thus exercise the muscles of questioning and exploring. Other topics, the tame ones — which seem to include some of the hoary old certainties of the curriculum — seem only to afford retention and comprehension (and while there is nothing wrong in exercising those muscles, one does not want too much of it, for verbatim recall is not a skill in the first rank of lifelong learning).[27]

Dispositions: the adverbs of the mind

Latent in everything I have been saying about the shift from Third to Fourth Generation approaches is a recognition that learning to learn involves more than skills. The educational world has recently been enchanted with the language of 'skills', 'competencies' and so on — we even have a government Department for Education and Skills. 'Skills' is a handy word, because it makes you believe that what students need to know, in addition to 'knowledge' and 'understanding', is something that can be dealt with through 'training'; and 'training', a word with strong connotations of animal conditioning and old-style industrial apprenticeships, is something that can be accomplished (a) over quite a short period, and (b) without attention to anything more 'personal'. To train someone to be a welder or a surgeon, you do not have to know about their hopes and fears. The language of 'skills' and 'training' smuggles in to our discussion of educational reform a very limited view of human nature and human learning.

... learning to learn involves more than skills.

We know that children's minds are not so easily boxed, however. How, and how well, they learn cannot be reduced to a matter of 'skill'; it involves their attitudes, values, interests and beliefs as well. Kamini believes that 'Maths isn't for girls' so she is not predisposed to try hard sums. Neither is Jack, but for a different reason: he believes that 'If you can't solve it in a minute, you can't solve it at all'. Leigh thinks that 'Bright people never have to try', so she feels stupid when she can't do something easily, and gives up too.

There is much more to literacy than merely the 'ability to read and write'. A 2003 survey by the National Foundation for Educational Research discovered that, as a result of five years of the Literacy Hour in primary schools, two things had happened. Levels of reading ability had gone up. And levels of reading enjoyment had gone down. 15% fewer 11-year-old boys enjoyed reading stories than five years previously – and this despite the Harry Potter phenomenon.[28] In the report of a similar study in the States, the author Rebecca Marcon offers one possible reason why skills and dispositions can shear apart:

> Later progress is slowed for most children when formal learning experiences are introduced too early. Pushing children too soon into 'formalised academics' can actually backfire when children move into later childhood grades where they are required to think more independently. This is because teacher-directed approaches that tell children what to do, when to do it and how to do it curtail the development of autonomy.[29]

To put it brutally: there are ways of going about raising standards that undermine the development of children's 'learning power'. They become more 'able', but less 'ready' and 'willing'. Forcing skill development can damage the disposition to learn. And anyone who tries to tell you that this important truth is 'pretentious gobbledegook' has quite failed to understand the fundamental nature of education.

Some people object to the word 'disposition'. They think 'dispositions' are mysterious psychic entities that muddy rather than clarify the picture of L2L. And perhaps the use of the word as a noun does invite this kind of unease. However it is easily avoided by thinking of 'dispositions' not as something separate from 'skills' or 'knowledge', but as indicators of the degree to which one is disposed to make use of that skill or knowledge. Rather than nouns, 'dispositions' are adverbs – those little signifiers of 'time, manner and place' that modify the verbs they accompany.

To be disposed to persist, for example, is simply

- to show persistence across a broad rather than a narrow range of occasions;
- to tend to persist in the face of more severe obstacles or frustrations; and
- to have a rich repertoire of ways of supporting and encouraging one's own persistence.

To be disposed to ask questions is to tend to ask questions in English as well as Design; and to ask questions despite a degree of discouragement from the teacher. When one is 'disposed' to self-evaluation – standing back from time to time and asking yourself how it is going – self-evaluation has become routine, second nature, and across the board.[30] Fourth Generation approaches to L2L are interested in fostering this deepening and strengthening of useful learning habits: nothing very mysterious about that. Indeed, the broadening, strengthening and deepening of the capabilities of effective learners – the systematic development of their 'learning power' – is perfectly capable of being evaluated and tracked.

> " *Fourth Generation approaches to L2L are interested in fostering this deepening and strengthening of useful learning habits.* "

Talking and modelling

Let me come back to the question of how teachers change as they move from G3 to Fourth Generation approaches to L2L. Through the example of the STUCK posters, I showed that the impact of such a simple tool depends on the teachers' being able to use it to support a change in the classroom climate. For it to work, they have to keep refreshing and enriching it, so that it fosters a cumulative shift in students' sense of purpose and identity. They move from believing 'We are here to learn stuff' to 'We are here to learn how to learn'; and from 'We are more or less successful *knowers*' to 'We are (all, whatever our level of attainment) developing *learners*'.

STUCK posters are just one small example of a host of ways in which teachers can alter the way they orchestrate and present activities, make use of displays on the walls, play with the nature of groupings, and so on, in order to develop learning power. Such aspects of classroom organisation are already at the front of teachers' minds — they are the kinds of things they are used to thinking about — and they are therefore an obvious place to start.

But inevitably, the consideration of how to support the development of learning power expands, in the reflective teacher's mind, from 'what I *arrange*' to include 'what I *say*' and 'how I *act*'. Sports coaches do not just set exercises and monitor progress; they inspire, motivate and enthuse; and they lead from in front. They know how important it is to practise what they preach. (That is why so many top coaches are ex-players and ex-athletes.) Just so, learning-power teachers tend to become interested in the beliefs and messages behind the way *they* talk and act.

The panels opposite give two illustrations of how such beliefs and messages can 'leak through' to students just from the way that teachers talk.

It is only a short step, for a committed L2L teacher, from the awareness of language to a broader reflection on what learning attitudes and dispositions she herself models in front of her students. Many of the teachers in the Cardiff project, for example, found themselves quite spontaneously saying 'I don't know' much more often. Some of them were rather disconcerted by this, for they had been trained to see any ignorance on their part as a chink in their professional armour. 'If I don't know the answer, won't the students lose respect for me?', they wondered. If education is all about being and becoming knowledgeable, this is a rational fear. But as soon as you extend your vision to include the goal of helping young people become better learners, it becomes blindingly obvious that hiding your own learning is exactly the wrong thing to do. How can students learn what it is like to think and learn like a scientist, or a poet, or a designer, if they never see their teachers thinking and learning, but only knowing?

The whole thrust of the fashionable discipline called 'cultural psychology' or 'sociocultural studies' is the realisation that — to sum up the message of Vygotsky into a slogan — 'You get your mind from your milieu'. In other words, mental and emotional habits are contagious, and therefore we tend, especially when young, to pick up the learning attitudes and strategies that are being modelled for us by the more experienced people we find ourselves observing and engaging with. G3 teachers thought they could get away with treating L2L as a matter of technique. Fourth Generation teachers know that it is more interesting, and potentially closer to home, than that.[31]

The power of language: aptitude or effort?

How do teachers interpret and comment on their students' successes, failures and struggles with learning? Professor Jacquelynne Eccles of the University of Michigan has shown, in extensive research, that these messages, whether delivered formally, through marking and reports, or informally in classroom conversation, have a direct, practical impact on students' development as learners. And there were striking differences in adults' attributions for boys and girls in different subjects. If a boy did well in maths, adults tended to feed back the idea that this was because he was 'bright' or 'good at figures', while if a girl did well, they were more likely to receive an 'effort attribution': 'Well done, sweetie; you must have worked really hard'.

Conversely, when a boy did badly, he was more likely to be told that he had not tried hard enough, while when a girl did poorly, she was often told that this meant she 'wasn't cut out for it'. (Interestingly, the pattern of attributions was reversed in English: if you like, you can work it through for yourself.) Furthermore, Eccles found that very quickly students took these attributions on board, so that a poorly-performing girl, for example, tended to withdraw her effort, on the (very rational) grounds that, if she was really 'not cut out for maths', there was no point in trying. Her resilience directly suffered. So if teachers are genuinely going to support students' learning development, they have to watch their tongues.[32]

The power of language: 'Could be' or 'Is'

Most overviews of 'learning power' agree that good learners are curious, creative and critical. They like to ask questions – they wonder 'How come ...?' They use their imaginations to explore possibilities – they wonder 'What if ... ?'. And they don't take things for granted – they tend to say 'Yes, but ...'. Obviously, if we value these dispositions and want young people to strengthen them, we have to invite their use. Professor Ellen Langer at Harvard has demonstrated a direct effect of one small but significant feature of teachers' language on students' willingness to display curiosity, creativity and criticality. When teachers are explaining something, if they talk as if whatever-it-is is unquestionably true, the 'three C's' are reduced. But if they add little phrases to their explanation like 'This is one way of looking at it', or 'Some people have suggested that it works like this', or even 'It could be like this' – then the three C's are engaged, and L2L can take place.

It is not rocket science to understand why this should be. If I tell you that something IS thus-and-so, what can you do with it? To put it more formally, what forms of learning are 'afforded' by the way I am speaking? Well, if it IS, then all you can do is do your best to understand and remember it, right? But if I tell you that it COULD BE, then immediately I am inviting you to think *how* else it could be. The simple shift in language opens up the space for you to be more questioning, imaginative, and thoughtful about whatever it is. Now, of course not everything is a 'could be'. If it's raining, it really is, and we need to take our raincoats. But every Fourth Generation teacher I have talked to is ready to admit that there could be much more room for COULD BE in her teaching than she had thought. In other words, she has unwittingly overused IS, and thereby, unintentionally, closed down her children's minds, and retarded their development as learners, more than she need have done.[33]

The L2L school as a whole

Let me just hint at a final jump that distinguishes the third from the Fourth Generation of L2L. G3 was all about the classroom. It was what individual teachers did to try to help their students achieve more. The Fourth Generation approaches spill out of the classroom into the life of the whole school — and beyond. If attitudes towards learning — asking questions, admitting difficulty and so on — are contagious, then presumably other people than your own teacher(s) can be useful 'carriers' of resilience, resourcefulness and so on, from whom one could catch them. What about the teaching assistants? The secretaries? The midday supervisors? What about people who might be invited in to the school to talk to the students about their learning experiences, in assemblies, for example? Why not have a programme of visits from people with interesting learning stories to tell — about learning to interpret the cries of their first child; about the fear and excitement of that first scuba dive; about coping with the first term at university; about starting a new business? Why not use assemblies to showcase some of the students' own out-of-school learning (as well as for 'celebrating success')?

What about helping the body of teachers as a whole to develop a stronger, more open learning culture for themselves? Why not encourage peer observation and mutual coaching? Why not have a slot in every staff meeting where teachers present something innovative in their practice to their colleagues? Why not look at the CPD policy to see how 'teachers-as-learners' could become more central, and more visible, in the life of the school? And what about the role of the leadership in the school? Could one of the key jobs of the headteacher be to 'walk the talk' of learning, making their own learning journeys, with all their ups and downs, more visible?

If students need rich activities that enable them to practise their developing learning habits, what about all the activities they can take part in outside lessons? How do playground supervisors encourage learning — as well as ensuring the children are safe? Can we strengthen the ethos of clubs, games, music groups and other out-of-hours activities so that students value stretching themselves above unadventurous success? What responsibilities are given to the (students') School Council, and how are its activities framed and monitored, so that students learn how to make best use of it? Is homework framed as an opportunity to develop the skills of independent learning, and as a site for investigating different aspects of 'how I learn best'?

5   Knitting the Strands of the Fourth Generation Together

As I have gone along, I have indicated some twelve ways – they conveniently form 12 C's – in which the Fourth Generation approaches to learning to learn are improving upon and going beyond those of the Third. Not all of these transformations are fully-fledged, by any means. Some of them are currently not much more than a question or an intention at the back of the mind. But they all represent significant progress; and together they form the basis of a powerful agenda for inquiry, innovation, research and change.

1   **Comprehensiveness.** Because Fourth Generation approaches are developing models of learning power that are broad and coherent, there is less likelihood of them falling into the G3 trap of mistaking the part for the whole (or the ear for the elephant). Whether it is Art Costa's 'seventeen habits of mind', the Australian PEEL project's 'twenty good learning behaviours', or Building Learning Power's range of 'learning muscles', there is wide agreement that effective learning depends upon qualities of attention; of emotional reactivity; of thought and imagination; of reflection and self-awareness; and of sociability and relationships.

2   **Credibility.** Fourth Generation L2L has to have a greater respect for the complexities of science, and resist the easy simplifications and the slogans. Learning cannot be reduced to sound-bites. Claims about the brain need to be subjected to special scrutiny.

3   **Challenge.** Fourth Generation approaches take on board the distinction between 'activity' and 'exercise'. Not all activity, however enjoyable, stretches and expands the system. Where some G3 practitioners thought that 'fun' was enough to produce L2L, we can now see that enjoyment and engagement are necessary but not sufficient conditions for L2L to occur. In the surveys, students don't say they want 'fun'. They want things that are real, interesting and *hard* to get their teeth into.

4   **Culture.** To achieve genuine L2L, the Fourth Generation approaches realise that they have to move beyond the 'hints and tips' stage, and think in terms of cultivation rather than training. Techniques are useful, but they achieve a qualitatively different kind of effect when they are used, developed and examined within an inquisitive L2L climate. L2L can't be bolted on to 'business as usual'; it has to shift the ethos.

5   **Communication.** Fourth Generation teachers know that, to create this climate, they need to attend to the kind of language they use to frame activities and comment (both formally and, more importantly, informally) on students' learning; and also to the messages that they convey through the way they respond, in front of the students, to all the kinds of learning that come their own way.

6 **Collaboration.** Where G3 approaches tended to be done *to* the students, Fourth Generation practitioners seem to value opportunities to become more and more transparent about L2L *with* their students, involving them (appropriately) in the questions and uncertainties of how to 'build learning power', rather than feeling obliged to deliver polished formulae. Students take on some responsibility for finding out how they can get better at learning.

7 **Criticism.** Fourth Generation teachers, and their students, are less passive or credulous in the face of L2L ideas than their G3 colleagues. They do not feel intimidated either by 'academic credentials' or fast-talking salesmanship. They see themselves as learners about L2L, and they know that learners often like to take time to think. They test out claims in their own practice. And they are not afraid to ask questions.

8 **Creativity.** Neither are Fourth Generation teachers afraid to take ideas and run with them, customising them for local conditions, capitalising on students' current interests, and developing them in all kinds of unanticipated ways. Approaches such as Building Learning Power offer schools a language and a framework for thinking about how to support L2L, but they leave a great deal of room for creative manoeuvre.

9 **Curriculum.** Where G3 approaches tended to talk of L2L as if it were a set of entirely content-free skills, the Fourth Generation acknowledges that many learning habits and skills are more or less content specific. Being an effective all-round learner means possessing both the generic habits, and specific ways of learning in more circumscribed domains. (A mechanic needs a multi-purpose socket set, *and* the particular set of tools that are needed to work on a Honda as opposed to a Ford.)

10 **Connections.** Where G3 approaches focused on the single teacher and the single classroom, Fourth Generation approaches assume that L2L strategies and policies need to join up across the whole school if they are to be most effective. There are vertical implications, for how students move through the years, and relate to students in different years; and horizontal implications, for how different subjects and activities are linked together to reinforce common messages and practices.

11 **Community.** L2L can influence the way a school relates to, and makes use of, the wider community in which it is set. Parents especially need to understand what L2L is about, and how they can support their own children's development as learners. Good beginnings on learning how to involve parents and community members in L2L have already been made.

12 **Carrying-over.** Finally, perhaps the most profound shift from G3 to the Fourth Generation is in the depth of schools' commitment to helping students develop habits, values, skills and dispositions that will be of use to them in the 'big wide world', as well as in the context of school attainment. G3 approaches used the rhetoric of lifelong learning, but tended in practice to slide back into focusing on traditional, more familiar priorities. Now there is a new resolve to see education as a preparation for a learning life; and a strengthening optimism that this goal can be pursued without a revolution, and without ditching Shakespeare!

6   Learning to Learn for Life: the Emerging New Vision for Schools

To conclude, let me just say a few more words on the twelfth C — Carrying-over. Behind many of the advances from the Third to the Fourth Generation of L2L lies a fundamental change of heart about what education is for. Schools have to deliver the goods in terms of examination results: it would be stupid to pretend otherwise. And, indeed, there are basic areas of knowledge and capability that we want young people to have mastered (though there is much less consensus about what exactly those are than there used to be).

But there is also a rapidly developing consensus that leaving school with a clutch of qualifications, and being able to read and write and calculate, is not enough. The changing nature of work means that lifelong learning, and the emotional resilience that goes with it, have become necessities rather than luxuries. The Internet has already transformed our access to knowledge. The problem is not how to find it, but how to select and evaluate what you need, and how to fend off the rest. Technologies of a million kinds, from liposuction to long-haul jets, from iPods to internet shopping, open up lifestyle possibilities undreamed of by our grandparents. Yet along with choice comes uncertainty, and the question is: how are we to help young people deal well with the fact-finding, the problem-solving and the decision-making — the life-crafting — that most of them will have to face, whether they want to or not?

The need for education to prepare all youngsters for life, and not just some for university, is widely agreed, and the rhetoric of lifelong learning is all around. Only a few people still think that 'learning to learn' is a nonsense, a distraction or a practical impossibility. But the earlier generations fell well short of providing young people with a genuine flying start on a learning life. They tinkered with classroom practice, and aimed, for lack of better understanding, at improving examination-oriented memory and comprehension. Nothing wrong with that — except that it is so much less than what youngsters need, and so far short of what the rhetoric was promising.

Now, with the help of a better appreciation of the sciences of learning — neuroscience, cognitive science and cultural psychology — and with the participation of innovative teachers in rapidly expanding numbers, we have a much clearer idea of how to turn the rhetoric into reality. Much practical wisdom already exists. And where we do not have answers — and there are many such places — we at least have better questions. The previous generations of learning-to-learn have been vital stepping stones on the way to a more sophisticated view. But they were provisional — as the Fourth will undoubtedly turn out to be — and progress will be impeded if the previous generations of pioneers are unwilling to move on. Mind maps and learning styles are not the Holy Grail of learning to learn.

There is a bigger, better-grounded, more ambitious game afoot.
And we are beginning to know how to play it.

References and notes

1   David Miliband, North of England Education Conference, January 2003.

2   Estyn, Her Majesty's Inspectorate for Education and Training in Wales, *Excellent School: A Vision for Schools in Wales in the 21st Century,* HMSO, 2003.

3   *Speaking Up, Speaking Out! The 2020 Vision Programme Research Report,* The Industrial Society: London, 1997.

4   It would be unfair to identify the authorship of this booklet. I shall be critical of it in a variety of respects, but it is no better or worse than dozens of publications, both commercial and in-house, that represent the third-generation approach.

5   Howard Gardner, *Frames of Mind: The Theory of Multiple Intelligences,* Basic Books: New York, 1983.

6   Howard Gardner, 'Multiple intelligences', keynote address, British Psychological Society Division of Educational and Child Psychology Annual Conference, York, January 1996.

7   Howard Gardner, quoted in Geoffrey and Rumela Caine, *Making Connections: Teaching and the Human Brain,* ASCD: Alexandria, VA, 1991, pp 32–33.

8   Howard Gardner, *Intelligence Reframed: Multiple Intelligences for the 21st Century,* Basic Books: New York, 1999, pp 141–142.

9   Robert Sternberg and Elena Grigorenko, 'Are cognitive styles still in style?', *American Psychologist,* 1997, vol. 52, pp 700–712.

10 Ibid.

11 Caroline Lodge, 'Investigating discourses of learning', doctoral dissertation, University of London Institute of Education, 2002.

12 Frank Coffield, 'Revealing figures behind the styles', *The Higher,* 2 January 2004, p 20. For an ironic take on 'learning styles', see Tim Homfray in the *Times Educational Supplement* of the same date, p 47.

13 P. Kenealy and A. Monsef, 'Music and IQ tests', *The Psychologist,* 1994, vol. 7, pp 346–348.

14 See for example Guy Claxton, *Building Learning Power,* TLO Limited: Bristol, 2002; Art Costa and Bena Kallick, *Habits of Mind,* ASCD: Alexandria, VA, 2000; Bill Lucas, *Power Up Your Mind,* Nicholas Brealey: London, 2002.

15 Carol Dweck, *Self-Theories: Their Role in Motivation, Personality and Development,* Psychology Press: Hove, 1999; Ted Thompson, 'Characteristics of self-worth protection in achievement behaviour', *British Journal of Educational Psychology,* 1993, vol. 63, pp 469–488.

16 For the evidence that such active reflection does raise attainment on national tests and exams, see Chris Watkins, 'Learning about learning enhances performance', *Research Matters,* No. 13, National School Improvement Network: London, Spring 2001.

17 Do not take my word for it. Dozens of action research projects carried out by teachers across all phases of education in Cardiff over the last three years make it plain that this shift is real, and brings with it improved behaviour, raised attainment, and a stronger appetite for learning. See *Learning to Learn: Enquiries into Building Resourceful, Resilient and Reflective Learners,* Vol. I (2002) and Vol. II (2003), published by City and County of Cardiff Schools Service. Copies available from Alice Griffith at AGriffith@cardiff.gov.uk.

18 Thanks are due to Ros Pollard, Beverley Brown, Alice Griffith and Hugh Knight for initiating this project and enabling it to continue.

19 Mike Forret, 'Learning electronics; an accessible introduction', D.Phil thesis, University of Waikato, Hamilton, New Zealand, 1998.

20 Stephen Fry, 'History Matters', speech at the public launch of the campaign 'History Matters – pass it on', July 2006: www.historymatters.org.uk and follow Media Centre / Press Releases. Also published in *The Observer*, July 9, 2006.

21 Diane Halpern, 'Teaching critical thinking for transfer across domains', *American Psychologist*, 1998, vol. 53, pp 449–455.

22 Chris Woodhead, *Class War: The State of British Education*, Little, Brown: London, 2002, pp 56–57.

23 Halpern, op. cit.; David Perkins and Gavriel Salomon, 'Are cognitive skills context-bound?', *Educational Researcher*, 1989, vol. 25, pp 16–25.

24 See for example Valerie Bayliss, *Opening Minds: Education for the 21st Century*, Royal Society of Arts: London, 1999.

25 For details on the changing face of 'intelligence', see Michael Howe, *IQ in Question*, Sage: London, 1997; Ken Richardson, *The Making of Intelligence*, Weidenfeld and Nicholson: London, 1999.

26 See note 14.

27 David Perkins, 'Building intelligent schools', public lecture sponsored by the British Council, Belfast, March 2002.

28 'Harry Potter fails to spread reading magic', *The Independent*, 3 December 2003.

29 Rebecca Marcon, 'Fourth-grade slump: the cause and cure', *Principal*, May 1995.

30 This way of looking at learning dispositions is spelled out in more detail in Guy Claxton and Margaret Carr, 'A framework for teaching learning: the dynamics of disposition', *Early Years*, in press.

31 See, for example, Jerome Bruner, *The Culture of Education*, Harvard University Press: Cambridge, MA, 1996; Michael Cole, *Cultural Psychology: A Once and Future Discipline*, Bellknap Press: Cambridge, MA, 1996; Gordon Wells and Guy Claxton (eds), *Learning for Life in the 21st Century: Sociocultural Perspectives on the Future of Education*, Blackwell: Oxford, 2002. The classic text is Lev Vygotsky, *Mind in Society*, Harvard University Press: Cambridge, MA, 1978.

32 Pamela Frome and Jacquelynne Eccles, 'Parents' influence on children's achievement-related perceptions', *Journal of Personality and Social Psychology*, 1998, vol. 74, pp 435–452.

33 Ellen Langer, *The Power of Mindful Learning*, Addison-Wesley: Reading, MA, 1997.

Other Fourth Generation books from Guy Claxton and TLO

Building Learning Power by Guy Claxton

International research into how the mind works shows that we are all capable of becoming better learners. *Building Learning Power* applies this research directly to the work of teachers in classrooms, to provide a practical framework for fostering lifelong learning in all young people. The book covers:

- How and when we learn best
- The new 'four Rs' - resilience, resourcefulness, reflectiveness and reciprocity
- The learning mind
- How teachers can lead others' learning, by seeing themselves as learning coaches rather than merely purveyors of knowledge
- How building learning power can combat the problems of disaffection, disengagement and disenchantment and increase achievement in tests and examinations
- The skills and understanding that will enable teachers to help young people become better learners
- How building learning power can be practically applied in schools and colleges

To prosper in the learning age, we must learn to embrace uncertainty with robust self-confidence, and approach the future with curiosity and optimism. *Building Learning Power* provides a clear direction for this exciting journey,

(120 pages, full colour.)

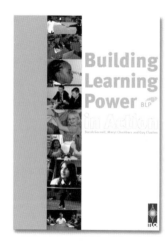

Building Learning Power in Action

by Sarah Gornall, Maryl Chambers and Guy Claxton

Building Learning Power in Action shows how some schools have embraced BLP, and captures the exciting effects it is having in classrooms. It describes a range of real live examples where busy teachers have tried out some aspects of BLP, and been (to put it mildly) pleasantly surprised by the results. In addition, it unpacks some of those stories, and gives a host of additional ideas about how you might achieve similar results.

"Term on term, year on year, a Building Learning Power school breeds young people who are more curious, more willing to take risks and give it a go, more imaginative and creative, more thoughtful, more ready, willing and able to learn with and from others. It's developing this adventurous spirit that counts."

(54 A4 pages, full colour.)

Building 101 Ways to Learning Power

by Maryl Chambers, Graham Powell and Guy Claxton

For teachers starting to explore learning power in their classrooms: *Building 101 Ways to Learning Power* encourages you to think that bit differently about how you can engage with your students in helping them to become better learners. The ideas grow out of Guy Claxton's *Building Learning Power,* offering practical ways for you to work with your class at exploring and expanding their learning capacities. However, don't expect an instruction manual, with detailed programmes and lists of tricks: there are lists, and classroom examples, and suggestions aplenty, but they aim to prompt and guide you into creating the ideas that will work with your students. Enjoy more rewards from your teaching as you coach your students in the processes of their own learning, with the shared knowledge that learning is learnable.

(28 A4 pages.)

Available from TLO Limited, Henleaze House, 13 Harbury Road, Bristol, BS9 4PN

OR Purchase electronically, or download an order form, at www.tloshop.co.uk

Building Learning Power™

The Fourth Generation programme from TLO

For schools who are committed to expanding their students' capacity to learn, we offer a growing range of publications, courses and conferences to stimulate and extend practice in Building Learning Power.

- — Enhance understanding and skills.
- — Ensure BLP principles are followed for full effect.
- — Encourage staff to explore and experiment.

We can tailor programmes and events to fit your local context.

Professor Guy Claxton acts as consultant, and chief inspiration, for this Building Learning Power programme. TLO Limited have worked closely with Professor Claxton since 2001: together we have sought to create a dynamic programme for translating his ideas into effective practice, in ways that can benefit every classroom and every young person. Schools, teachers and children have participated in every stage of this exciting journey of development.

For more details, contact:

TLO Limited   t: 0117 989 8204
Henleaze House
13 Harbury Road   e: info@tloltd.co.uk
Bristol
BS9 4PN   w: www.buildinglearningpower.co.uk
                   www.tloltd.co.uk

Photo credits